Passive Income

Web Business & Internet Marketing

2 in 1 Bundle

Live the Life of Your Dreams with these Proven Online Business Ideas & Effective Marketing Strategies

By

Julie Rausch

Would you like more **FREE** tips and resources to help you achieve online success and wealth?

Please go to the below link for my **FREE** offer:

"Easy Marketing Tips for Your Home-Based Business"

http://eepurl.com/c8rgw5

Or visit my website:

www.julierausch.wix.com/author

To sign up

© Copyright 2017 by JRPublishingGroup - All rights reserved.

No part of this book may be reproduced or distributed in any form without permission in writing from the author. Reviewers may quote brief passages in reviews.

The following eBook is reproduced below with the goal of providing information that is as accurate and as reliable as possible. Regardless, purchasing this eBook can be seen as consent to the fact that both the publisher and the author of this book are in no way experts on the topics discussed within, and that any recommendations or suggestions made herein are for entertainment purposes only. Professionals should be consulted as needed before undertaking any of the action endorsed herein.

This declaration is deemed fair and valid by both the American Bar Association and the Committee of Publishers Association and is legally binding throughout the United States.

Furthermore, the transmission, duplication or reproduction of any of the following work, including precise information, will be considered an illegal act, irrespective whether it is done electronically or in print. The legality extends to creating a secondary or tertiary copy of the work or a recorded copy and is only allowed with express written consent of the Publisher. All additional rights are reserved.

The information in the following pages is broadly considered to be a truthful and accurate account of facts, and as such any inattention, use or misuse of the information in question by the reader will render any resulting actions solely under their purview. There are no scenarios in which the publisher or the original author of this work can be in any fashion deemed liable for any hardship or damages that may befall them after undertaking information described herein.

Additionally, the information found on the following pages is intended for informational purposes only and should thus be considered, universal. As befitting its nature, the information presented is without assurance regarding its continued validity or interim quality. Trademarks that mentioned are done without written consent and can in no way be considered an endorsement from the trademark holder.

CONTENTS

INTRODUCTION 1

CHAPTER ONE: WHY START AN ONLINE BUSINESS? 3
    MONEY 3
    FAMILY 4
    SELF-ESTEEM 4
    TAX BENEFITS 5
    SAVINGS 5
    FLEXIBILITY 5
    YOU ARE YOUR BOSS 6
    THINK OF IT AS AN INVESTMENT 6
    IT IS NOT EXPENSIVE 6

CHAPTER TWO: OVERCOMING ANY HURDLES 8
    STOCKING INVENTORY 8
    THE CAPITAL REQUIRED 8
    TECHNICAL ASPECTS 9
    BRAND REPUTATION 9
    SEO STRATEGY 9
    TARGET AUDIENCE 10
    PAYMENT GATEWAY 10
    CUSTOMER SERVICE 10

CHAPTER THREE: TARGET AUDIENCE 11
    YOUR BUSINESS PLAN 11
    RESEARCH, RESEARCH, AND RESEARCH 12
    DEVELOPING THE CUSTOMER PROFILE 12

LOCATE YOUR AUDIENCE 13

MONITOR AND EVOLVE 13

CHAPTER FOUR: BE AN EXPERT – BUILD A BRAND 14

LOTS OF RESEARCH 14

YOUR BRAND NEEDS A VOICE 15

BALANCING YOUR MEDIA MIX 15

SOCIAL MEDIA INTEGRATION 16

BUILDING YOUR REPUTATION ONLINE 16

CHAPTER FIVE: SUCCESS MINDSET 17

DEFINING SUCCESS 17

SET GOALS FOR YOURSELF 17

FIND SOME INSPIRATION 18

CREATE HABITS THAT COMPLIMENT YOUR GOALS 18

CREATE A ROUTINE BASED ON THOSE HABITS 18

STOP PROCRASTINATING 19

SUCCESS ISN'T THAT DISTANT 19

CHAPTER SIX: MARKET YOUR ONLINE BUSINESS 20

SEARCH ENGINE OPTIMIZATION 20

PAY-PER-CLICK ADVERTISING 21

PUBLISHING AN E-NEWSLETTER 21

START A BLOG 22

SOCIAL MEDIA 22

POSITIVE CUSTOMER REVIEWS 22

OTHER TIPS 23

CHAPTER SEVEN: AFFILIATE MARKETING 25

BUILD YOUR WEBSITE TRAFFIC FIRST, AND BE PATIENT .. 25

ONE GOOD PRODUCT OR BUSINESS IS ENOUGH 26

- CONTENT IS VERY IMPORTANT 28
- PROMOTE YOUR SITE 30
- DON'T BE INVISIBLE OR ANONYMOUS 32

CHAPTER EIGHT: BLOGGING 34
- SETTING UP A BLOG 34
- USEFUL CONTENT 34
- FIND READERS 35
- BUILDING ENGAGEMENT 36
- START MAKING MONEY 37
- WHILE BLOGGING, KEEP THESE SIMPLE THINGS IN MIND. 39

CHAPTER NINE: VLOGGING 40

CHAPTER TEN: VIRTUAL ASSISTANT 44
- GENERAL OR ADMINISTRATIVE VIRTUAL ASSISTANTS 44
- DIGITAL MARKETING VIRTUAL ASSISTANTS 45
- PROGRAMMING VIRTUAL ASSISTANTS 45
- DESIGN VIRTUAL ASSISTANTS 45
- WRITING VIRTUAL ASSISTANTS 46
- A/V EDITING VIRTUAL ASSISTANTS 46
- FINANCIAL VIRTUAL ASSISTANTS 46

CHAPTER ELEVEN: FREELANCE WRITER/TRANSCRIBER 48
- STARTING A BLOG 48
- PITCHING A GUEST POST 48
- YOUR ALMA MATER 49
- WRITING A LISTICLE 49
- SELF-PUBLISHING A BOOK 50
- SIGNING UP FOR A CONTENT SITE 50
- BECOMING A COPYWRITER 50

- WRITING FAN-FICTION 51
- **CHAPTER TWELVE:** AMAZON FBA 52
  - WHAT IS FBA? 52
  - WORKING WITH FBA 52
  - FBA IN MOTION 53
    - SENDING PRODUCTS TO AMAZON 53
    - RECEIPT AND STORING OF GOODS BY AMAZON 54
    - REQUESTS FOR ORDERS 54
    - PRODUCTS ARE PICKED AND PACKED 54
    - SHIPPING OF PRODUCTS 55
  - THINGS NEEDED 56
    - A SMARTPHONE 56
    - A SCOUTING APP 56
    - A PRINTER 56
    - PACKAGING EQUIPMENT 56
- **CHAPTER THIRTEEN:** SELL YOUR KNOWLEDGE 57
  - E-BOOK OR A WHITE PAPER 57
  - A SEMINAR OR A CLASS 58
  - TUTORING 58
  - WRITING FOR WEBSITES 58
  - CONSULTING SERVICES 59
  - ANSWERING QUESTIONS 59
- **CHAPTER FOURTEEN:** NICHE STORES ON EBAY, SHOPIFY 60
  - FIND A NICHE 60
  - SELECT A PRODUCT 61
  - YOUR COMPETITION 61
  - SETTING UP YOUR STORE 61

PRICING YOUR PRODUCT	62
COMPOSE PRODUCT PHOTOS	63
COMPOSE TITLES	64
CHAPTER FIFTEEN: DIRECT SALES - WHAT IT TAKES	66
COMPANY STRATEGY	67
A PRODUCT THAT EXCITES YOU	67
ATTITUDE MATTERS	68
GOOD AT NETWORKING	68
INTRODUCTION TO INTERNET MARKETING	69
IMPACT OF SOCIAL MEDIA	72
FACEBOOK	76
TWITTER	84
INSTAGRAM	89
YOUTUBE	93
PINTEREST	96
WEBSITE DESIGN STRATEGIES	102
EMAIL MARKETING	115
ONLINE PROMOTIONS	129
CONCLUSION	132

Introduction

The Internet has managed to revolutionize all aspects of our lives, and the world of trade and commerce is no exception. You no longer need to be physically present to conduct your business. You can do so from the comfort of your own home! Web businesses are not only quite lucrative, but they also provide you the opportunity of doing something that you enjoy!

For years, I sat at a desk in a cubicle, working the daily nine-to-five grind in the insurance industry. I secretly dreamed of having my own business. I went back to school to become an aesthetician and did that for 14 years. I loved it because I was up and about, not tied to a desk, and meeting a lot of new people. Although I enjoy the aesthetics profession, I still longed for my own business, a business where I could be my boss and work from home or anywhere for that matter, as long as I had my laptop. Through discovering my strengths and passions, and the explosion in Internet opportunity, my dreams of having my own business online came to fruition. And now I would like to encourage other people and share how to be successful with their own online business.

In this book, you will learn about web businesses, the benefits they offer, tips for creating the right attitude for becoming a successful entrepreneur, and the different ideas for starting your own business online. There are various options to choose from like content writing, blogging, affiliate marketing, FBA, vlogging, and so much more. You will find helpful tips and steps that you can follow for starting your own online business. So, are you ready to get started?

Chapter One:

Why Start an Online Business?

There is no time like the present to start your own business, and it has never been as easy as it is today. With the invention of social media and the advent of social media, you can connect with anyone regardless of their geographical location. Regardless of your social status, now you can share your skills and connect with people across the globe. If you are thinking about starting your own online business, it is quite economical and easy to get started. In fact, you can start your business for less than a $100 (yes, that's the cost of acquiring a domain name and a hosting service). If you can connect with your potential audience, you can indeed start your own business. There are plenty of benefits of starting your own online business. In this chapter, I have listed these benefits.

Money

Money is necessary, and it does make the world go around. We would all like to have some more of it though, wouldn't we? Whether it is for debt repayment, saving for retirement, or just for making ends meet, with the right knowledge, an online business can help you in earning money almost immediately. Unlike a conventional job, you needn't restrict yourself to just one avenue. You can select multiple avenues and work on all of them simultaneously. For instance, you can be a freelance writer, a blogger and an affiliate marketer! It depends on the time and effort you are willing to put into it.

Family

Let's be realistic now. If you are married and have children, then you will have your regular household chores to manage as well. It is not just your career, but your family that needs your time as well. A job that allows you to work from the convenience of your own home enables you to spend more time with your family!

Self-esteem

Most of us are so busy being mothers, wives and members of the community that we tend to forget that our lives are a reflection of our inner-selves. Starting your own business is a big accomplishment and something to be proud of; it will help in boosting your self-esteem and make you more confident as well.

Tax benefits

Most of the women who start an online business are doing it from their homes. They will be eligible for significant tax deductions for starting their home business. Fewer taxes mean more significant savings for you!

Savings

This is an obvious one. If you are working from home, then you don't have to splurge on expensive formal wear for your work. Women spend over $150 for an average professional suit! Can you imagine not having to buy expensive clothes for work anymore? Also, if you are working from home, you can conveniently cook your meals and brew your coffee. All these things might seem trivial but, over a period, you will be able to save a lot of money by not having to buy these things elsewhere.

Flexibility

You get to decide when and how you would like to work. There is no assigned workspace that you need to show up at. You can also work while you are traveling! All you need is your laptop and a good Internet connection, and you are good to go! This also means that you can spend more time with your loved ones. You can take a day off whenever you feel like it. You have the power to decide how much work you are willing to take on and the amount you want to make. You no longer have to worry about being paid less than your actual worth, and you don't have to ask anyone for a raise. With the right knowledge, persistence and hard work, you can generate as much income as you want to.

You are your boss

You don't have to worry about layoffs. Who will fire you, when you are your boss? You have the power to make all the decisions. This doesn't mean that there aren't any risks, but you can at least control what you are doing, and you aren't at someone else's mercy anymore.

Think of it as an investment

If you manage to build a successful online business for yourself, you can always sell it in the future and profit off of your hard work.

It is not expensive

As I mentioned earlier, numerous small businesses started building their business empires with just a domain name and a hosting service for housing their business website.

Start an online business, because you want to do something for yourself and not because of what someone else says.

Chapter Two:

Overcoming Any Hurdles

There are a couple of hurdles that you might face while starting a web business of your own. In this chapter, you will learn about these hurdles and how you can turn them in your favor.

Stocking inventory

It is important to keep stock of your inventory if you have an online store. A little extra inventory is helpful but too much of it might go to waste, and it will just increase your expenses. Before you can think about becoming an online seller, you must research the niche you are catering to and understand the demand for the product you are thinking about selling. When you have these metrics at hand, you can maintain your inventory levels accordingly.

The capital required

Regardless of the business you are thinking about starting, capital is required. Capital is the initial investment you will need to make for starting your own business. You don't need to invest a lot in starting your web business. However, remember that profits might not be instantaneous, and you will need to prepare yourself financially. Research and analyze the market before taking the plunge.

Technical aspects

If you are a web or a graphic designer, then you are certainly equipped to design your website. However, if you have no idea about designs, then you should hire some help for doing so. You don't have to do everything by yourself. You might do more harm than good to your business if you aren't sure of the technical aspects involved in starting a web business.

Brand reputation

This is perhaps one of the biggest fears an e-commerce business owner could harbor. Make use of social media for engaging with your customers. The more you engage and the more attention you pay to what they like and dislike, the better your chances of improving your reputation.

SEO strategy

As and when your website, vlog, or blog is ready, you need to have a good SEO or digital marketing strategy in place. SEO helps in improving your online visibility, and this is extremely important for an online business.

Target audience

Who is your target audience? Do plenty of research to understand the market you are targeting and the demand for the product or service that you are offering. If there is no demand for what you are offering, then the chances of your success are going to be quite low.

Payment gateway

There are multiple payment options to choose from, and as a business owner, you are supposed to select a payment gateway that your target audience is comfortable with. You can opt for wire transfers, PayPal, credit or debit cards, and so on.

Customer service

Providing good customer service is essential for any business. If a customer is satisfied with the service you provide, it is likely that they will come back. If they aren't, then the chances of bad publicity tend to increase as well. Keep collecting feedback and make the required changes for improving your customer service.

Chapter Three:

Target Audience

If you were just starting your business, then you would have spent a lot of time planning and building it. A significant part of this process is deciding who will be on the receiving end of all the efforts you are making. The product or service you are offering is as important as the target audience. As a business owner, you will want to have as many customers as possible. In this chapter, you will learn about finding your target audience.

Your business plan

Start by taking a look at the goals you have set for yourself and carefully analyze the products or services that you are offering. Think about the need or the problem that your products or services will help in fulfilling or solving. Also, think about the defining factor that will differentiate your business from that of your competitors. Think about the information you require and the need for the same. What do you need to know about your target audience for reaching them? Consult your business plan and decide who your target audience is. Don't think about the people you would want to sell to. Instead, think about all those who are looking for the product or the service that you are offering.

Research, research, and research

Secondary research is important. There are plenty of sources that you can gather information from about the industry, niche, competitors, and target audience that you are looking at. Secondary research involves using information that someone else has already gathered and you don't have to do all the research again. However, don't depend on it entirely. Do some research of your own as well.

Developing the customer profile

Once you have completed your research, you must create a customer profile. This is so much more than just a simple statement. It is a detailed description of who your likely customers will be and include certain demographic and psychographic information about them. It can involve data about the potential customer's age, gender, location, income, and other demographic information and psychographic information like hobbies, interests, attitudes, and so on. This information is quintessential for developing your customer profile. Demographic information will help you in identifying who your customer is, and psychographic information assists in determining why the customer needs your product or service.

Locate your audience

Your work doesn't stop after identifying your target audience. You need to find the websites and social media networks they frequently use. Get involved and form a presence for yourself by posting on these websites and social media sites. Do they like checking their emails or is there a particular app that they love to use? Make use of all this information and combine it with the customer profile, and you can locate your customers.

Monitor and evolve

Once you have identified your target audience, you will need to keep researching continuously for understanding the current market trends and your competition in the industry. Keep track of how your customer is evolving. Before you start marketing, you need to know how you plan on tracking the sales, interactions, requests for information, and other data.

Chapter Four:

Be an Expert – Build a Brand

Investing in your brand online is a crucial step since it allows you to create an entity that will resonate with your customers and keep them coming back for more. Building your brand online will help you in improving the awareness and reputation of your brand. The more people that are invested in your brand; the greater are the chances of your customers staying loyal. If you are interested in the growth of your online business, you will need to work on the growth of your brand. Here are five things that you should keep in mind if you are interested in building your brand on the Internet.

Lots of research

The first step in building your brand is to have a thorough understanding of your target audience, especially before you start creating strategies for content and communication. There are plenty of online tools that you can make use of for identifying your target audience. Make use of the information provided it the previous chapter to identify your target audience.

Your brand needs a voice

Depending on the research, you can determine what your audience would want to her and the message you would want to put forth. This will help in establishing the foundation for your brand. While you are doing this, you will need to keep a couple of things in mind. Always keep an open mind and consider all the ideas that before selecting one. While creating and developing content, you should speak with your audience and check the topics that they can relate to and the information that keeps them engaged.

Balancing your media mix

You should make use of different channels for building your brand. Make use of content and display networks to publicize about your brand through repletion and make use of behavioral marketing for targeting your audience. From the perspective of organic search, your brand name and message should be consistent with the title tags and Meta descriptions you use. Your message should be in perfect harmony with your brand's voice. Consistency is key to improving your brand's visibility.

Social media integration

What are the kind of interactions you would want your customers to have with your business? What would you want your brand to convey on social media? What is the right social media platform for you? You might not have all the answers right away, but with a little research, you will be able to understand where your audience is located and how you can improve your interaction with them.

Building your reputation online

It is quite similar to networking, but it does take some time and effort. You will need to have a well-defined strategy that you can make use of to reach out to your target audience. The next step is to identify all the different tactics that you can use. For instance, you can leverage any of the existing offline partnerships that you might have for growing your online reputation.

Chapter Five:

Success Mindset

Having the right attitude matters as much as the work that you are doing, if you want to achieve success. In this chapter, you will learn about the seven steps that you can follow for achieving success from the inside out.

Defining success

If you don't define what success means to you, then you will keep subjecting yourself to confusion about what is a success and what is a failure. Think about what is important to you in your personal and professional lives. Take a while, set your ego and guilt aside, and think what your idea of a "perfect life" is.

Set goals for yourself

Now that you know what success personally means to you, you need a plan for achieving that success. Without a plan or a strategy, you will never be successful. So, you must start setting goals for yourself.

Find some inspiration

Setting goals does not serve any purpose if you don't convince your brain to stick to those goals. Look for something that inspires you and motivates you. You can read inspirational books, watch motivational videos, or visualize what you would feel after achieving your goals. Really get in touch with those good feelings that would follow manifestation of your dreams and goals. These things will keep you going, even when things seem impossible and tough.

Create habits that compliment your goals

Setting goals work well when you develop habits surrounding those goals. There is a direct relationship that exists between your goals and the rate of depletion of motivation. If you aren't habitual in doing things for achieving your goals, then your motivational levels are bound to plummet.

Create a routine based on those habits

Successful people know how to live their success, regardless of whether others notice it or not. You must learn to live your success. Always put your best foot forward and do the best you can. Tackle all the tough tasks that come your way and don't give up.

Stop procrastinating

Routines are essential and not having one will lead to wastage of time and effort. There will be times when you will feel dejected and feel like nothing is working in your favor. Or there might be times when you don't feel like doing something, and everything seems pointless. In such cases, you need to stop procrastinating and get on with your work. Take a break if you feel like it, but don't postpone your work.

Success isn't that distant

Stop thinking that success is a distant achievement. It is as distant as you perceive it to be. Stop wishing for success and start doing things that will help you in achieving the success you have been dreaming of!

Chapter Six:

Market Your Online Business

Having a website alone doesn't do the trick anymore. If you want to increase your rate of success, then you need to learn about marketing your business online. In this chapter, you will learn about different things you can do for increasing the visibility of your website, generating more traffic, and increasing your sales.

Search engine optimization

The basis of SEO is to write the website copy in such a manner that your website will appear high on the result pages of popular search engines when a user uses a specific keyword for searching. You can make use of the services offered by different companies for optimizing your site. Well, you can try your hand at SEO if you want to. Think of a couple of simple words or phrases that a customer might make use of while searching for a business similar to yours, and then type it into any of the popular search engines like Google or Bing. You will receive results for similar phrases that were searched. Pick a longer phrase and a couple of keywords, and use them in the copy of your website's home page.

Pay-per-click advertising

SEO and Pay-per-click are often clubbed together as a tool for increasing the traffic to a given website. However, these two aren't similar and are quite different. When it comes to PPC, you can purchase a couple of keywords and phrases from a search engine based on pay-per-click. For instance, let us assume that you are selling skateboards in a particular city. If you purchase the keyword phrase "skateboards in ____ city," an ad for your website will appear in the "paid results" section of the search. Whenever someone clicks on such a link, they would be redirected to your website, and you will need to pay a pre-decided fee to the search engine.

Publishing an e-newsletter

You can drive traffic to your website by publishing e-newsletters. When this is done properly, it will enable you to reach your target audience consistently and direct them to your website for more information about your business, the products or services offered, and so on. The secret to publishing a good e-newsletter is to develop a database carefully and to provide some valuable content to the target audience instead of a poorly veiled sales pitch. Also, the recipients should have the option of opting out of the newsletter whenever they want to.

Start a blog

You can improve the rankings of your website by writing a blog. Write a blog and post the links to your website in it. This will help in diverting some traffic to your website. You can use the same keywords and keyword phrases in your blog as you did for your website.

Social media

Social media platforms are primarily meant for socializing. However, their function isn't just limited to that. You can make use of social media to promote and market your business online. This is the best manner in which you can connect with your target audience. You can make use of social media to divert web traffic to your website as well. You can start a Facebook page or group and do Facebook Ads to gain members.

Positive customer reviews

Whenever you buy something online, do you look at the reviews that a particular seller has received? Would you be comfortable while buying products from a seller on Amazon with two stars or with four stars? You would obviously choose a seller with positive customer reviews. Not just that, there are plenty of websites that help in posting reviews online. Make sure that you reply positively to a comment posted by a customer regardless of whether it is positive or not.

Other tips

Even if the idea of getting started with online marketing seems daunting, do not panic. It might seem tricky, but it is simple. You have already done the most difficult thing: leaping into an unknown territory by starting your own business! Kudos on that and don't lose your nerve now! Don't expect any immediate results. Spend some time and create an online marketing strategy that can work in your favor. You just need to spend about 2 to 4 hours every week doing this. You can start by acquiring a URL for your web business. There are plenty of services to choose from and buy an online name that is suitable for your business. You can always personalize it in some form. Once you have a URL, the next step is to decide on the kind of technology you are inclined towards. You can make use of a conventional website or a blog-style website. Wix.com, Godaddy.com, and Wordpress.com are excellent sites for beginners. You will need to set up a storefront for your web business. It doesn't have to be anything jazzy; you can try the minimalistic route instead.

Like I already mentioned, don't underestimate the power of keywords and keyword phrases. This is the best way to direct web traffic to your website. The reviews your business receives needn't always be favorable. At times, you can receive unfavorable reviews as well. When this happens, make sure that you handle it professionally and don't let your emotions dictate an answer. Make the most of social media and create social media presence for your web business! Also, remember that you don't have to do everything on your own. It is okay to ask for help. If you feel that you need help with any aspect of starting and running a business, join entrepreneurial groups on Facebook or groups that are similar to your niche, or seek mentors and professional help.

Chapter Seven:

Affiliate Marketing

One of the easiest ways in which you can make money online is by taking up affiliate marketing. You don't have to work on product ideas, product creation, providing customer support, or any other problems that are associated with the creation and development of a product. All that you need to do is just promote a product.

Build your website traffic first, and be patient

Affiliate marketing thrives on people's interest in clicking on links to products that catch their eye. But who are these "people"? All those who visit your blog or website to read what you have written. So, make your blog or site as interesting as possible, if you are interested in luring them. Remember that you need to establish a good reader base to land an affiliate marketing gig. Your content should be as engaging as the look of your blog or website.

If you're not getting a good number of unique to your website, you're not going to get the click-through to your affiliate. Here, "unique" refers to new customers and not the same old ones who have probably bookmarked and keep visiting all the time. The traffic to your blog or site increases when the number of people visiting it is going to increase. Not everyone is going to click on the links, and to get a reasonable number of clicks; you need plenty of regular visitors. You also need to build up a reputation as an expert in your niche before people trust you enough to go for your recommendations. There should be interesting content for people to read and remain glued. It is not helpful if they visit just once and immediately forget about your blog. You need to track the number of people that visit your page and record the numbers per day, month and year. This will help you in knowing how popular your blog is.

One good product or business is enough

Now that we understood who these "people" are, it will help you in generating good traffic come your way, let us look at what they will be interested in.

Newcomers to the system often make the mistake of peppering their site or sites with lots of different things, imagining that people are likely to buy more because they have more choices. It is typical human thinking to want a lot of choices in anything and everything, let alone links on a website. You are not a store – you don't have to offer your customers choices because they did not land on your site with purchase in mind. They're there for information, and if you're good at what you do, you'll be able to persuade them to buy something while they are there so that you can make some cash.

Think of it as a classy gig to have only one website promotion, and that website is the best one that your readers can have. That is, you will have the chance to promote one product or service better rather than having to do it for five or six different ones. Not only will that confuse your customers but will confuse you as well. You will have to look into two or three different companies and think of where their links will look the best. Think of yourself as a pop-up store to promote one product as opposed to a supermarket that offers a lot of choices.

The power of suggestion works for a majority of the customers. They will take a liking to something if you tell them that you are offering them the same product that you have personally tested and liked yourself.

Don't make the mistake of putting up too many choices at once. If you have put up just one product and the website is offering it at the best price in the market then even if the person has left your site to do a quick price comparison, he or she is sure to return to yours to click on the ad. Also, focusing on a single product or business makes it easier to make keywords work for you. So, stick with one business or product. If you want to do more, set up a different website for each affiliate, and concentrate on that, rather than spreading yourself too thin. What you can then do is, try and link your sites.

Content is very important

This is true of any website of course, but it's especially relevant if you are hoping to make money from affiliate marketing. People go to websites to be informed or entertained – often both at the same time. So, make sure you have plenty of content structured around the products or business you are promoting.

Another point to remember is that search engines can tell whether there's quality content on your site, and will rank it higher as a result. That means more visitors and hopefully more sales. You must be well versed in the concept of "SEO." SEO refers to search engine optimization. You must have heard that many companies have a good SEO team which helps them in becoming popular. Well, this is true because these teams will work hard on promoting the websites and blogs of the company and help it appear on top of the Google search list.

You should pick out all the top words from your blog or website, which are most likely going to be typed by people. If they get the combination of words right, then your site is going to appear as the topmost links. For this, you can also make use of a small description that will help you put in all the main words.

But remember just a good SEO description will not do the trick, and you need to have a good content as well. So, forget about the keyword-stuffed sales pitches when you are coming up with the content for your blog – educate, inform, entertain, but whatever you do, don't spam. You don't need long articles – in fact, three hundred-word posts will hold the attention of your audience better than one 800 to 900-word post. The more information you give away, the better the reader base. Most people will look for sites that will give them an in-depth look at difficult topics. By making it easy for them, you will have a chance to increase your reader base.

You need to be as different and unique as possible. For instance, if you wish to provide customers with recipe ideas then come up with good and unique ones that are not easily available on the Internet. Once they take a liking to your unique recipes, they will be interested in clicking on an ad on your site, which might be a particular cream cheese brand or even baking trays. You can also explicitly mention that you have used these brands and hyperlink the products with the words. Your readers are sure to click on them!

Keep the posts on the topic, and plant the idea in the reader's mind that they need to buy whatever you're promoting. You can even drop a contextual link to a particular product in the content. Help them reach a decision, rather than trying to direct them straight to the sales site. The soft approach is the best approach here as you are trying to be subtle about your promoting. I am sure you have bought many things by clicking on ads put up on blogs and sites that you read.

Promote your site

This sounds obvious, but if you want people to come to your site, read your content and click on your affiliate links, you need to let them know the site exists. Whether it is a product or a service, everything needs to be promoted for people to be aware of what you are doing. Without proper promotion, how are people going to get word about your website out there? There are only so many friends that will click on your links and for you to land a big gig; you will need at least 1000 clicks a week.

Firstly, list your site in search engines, write press releases to be distributed online, and promote your site on forums in your niche and social media.

If you have a friend whose blog is extremely popular, then you can consider asking him or her to subtly promote yours on theirs. But you might have to consider paying them a small fee for it, as you will be benefitting from their service to you. If you don't have any such friends but know of someone who has such a blog, then you can consider contacting them and asking them politely to promote yours. It's a good idea to have Facebook and Twitter account linked to your website and set up so that each time you post an update on the site, it's posted to your social media account. You can also have a Facebook page dedicated to your website or blog where you will keep updating with links to your site. Work on building an army of followers, but don't even consider buying them. Bought followers are not going to go to your website and click on the affiliate links – they just give an illusion that your social media account is more popular than it is.

You might think of being popular but once the bubble bursts, you might be extremely disappointed. If it is a group of friends, then make sure the group is genuinely interested in your blog or site and are not just doing you a favor. Those will only last for a while and decide to abandon you once they lose interest.

Don't be invisible or anonymous

This is a golden rule. First and foremost, you must have confidence in who you are and what you do. If you don't have self-confidence, then it will not work in your favor. Just because it's easy to hide behind an alias on the Internet, it doesn't mean you should. It can be tempting to use a cool name but don't do so. If you want to build credibility and earn money online, you have to be seen as a real person, with proper contact details. Don't hide behind a pen name or a nickname, use a real name and an email address tied to your domain name, rather than a Hotmail or an AOL account. If you wish to use a pen name, then consider putting it in brackets so that the person is aware of your real name as well. Make sure you write out your full name including initials, as there can be many others with the same name as you. Remember that people need to know they can contact you with questions and that they will get an answer from a real person. They might also ask for a genuine photograph just to be sure of who the other person is. If they can't trust the Webmaster, they're not going to click on the affiliate link, and you won't make any money. It's all about trustworthiness.

Before you start to make money from affiliate marketing, you need to have your site set up to encourage people to click through on the advertising links. That means having great content that's informative and entertaining, earning a reputation for being an expert in your niche and taking a soft approach to selling. Let your knowledge and enthusiasm persuade the reader to click through, rather than filling the site with banners and sales pitch. Also, be sure to provide proper contact details, so your readers know you are a real person.

Chapter Eight:

Blogging

In this chapter, you will learn about making money by becoming a blogger! Blogging is fun if you like writing and sharing on social media. Here is how to make money from a blog.

Setting up a blog

Well, this one is pretty obvious, isn't it? You cannot possibly make money by becoming a blogger if you don't have a blog! Blogging is simple, and you don't have to feel intimidated or overwhelmed at the thought of creating your blog. You can start by creating your blog on WordPress if you want to.

Useful content

You cannot have a successful blog without posting any useful content. Your primary focus should be on churning out content that others would want to read about. Take some time and select a topic. Once you have done this, you can start writing about it. The key to becoming a successful blogger is by catering to the needs of a niche or a particular demographic. The content that you create should be useful to your audience.

It doesn't have to change their lives necessarily, but it certainly should add some value!

Find readers

Once you have started writing and creating useful content, you should start focusing on building your reader base. Most of the bloggers tend to have a "build it, and readers will automatically come to" mentality, but this is nothing but a trap. If you are interested in making money from your blog, then your focus shouldn't be just on building a great blog, but also on having a good number of followers as well. So, you need to get off the blog and start promoting your blog! There are different ways in which you can experiment with increasing your blog's audience. You need to be able to divert and retain traffic that comes to your blog. The first step is to think about the kind of readers you would like to have read your blog. You can create a reader profile, and this will help in attracting the kind of audience that you are looking for. Once you know the kind of audience you want, you can start looking for places where such audience would gather. Start by listing down answers to these questions:

- Are they reading any specific blogs? Make a note of the top 3 blogs.

- Are they participating in any forums? Make a note of the top 3 forums.

- The social networking platforms they are active on? Make a note of the top 3 social networking media for this purpose.

- Are they listening to any podcasts? If yes, then list the top 3 podcasts.

These are great places for attracting the kind of readers that you want. Now that you are aware of where to find your target audience, you need to make the most of these platforms and make your presence felt. Keep building awareness about your blog and increase your audience base.

Building engagement

When you start focusing on creating good and useful content and finding readers for your blog, you will start noticing that people are not just visiting your blog, but they are engaging with the content of it as well. When this starts happening, you will need to concentrate on engaging with your audience as well and building yourself a community of readers and followers. Respond to all the comments that they post and keep them engaged. Keep them coming back for more.

Start making money

Once you have started your blog, created good content, found readers, and have started engaging with them, the next step is to start making money from your blog. Monetizing your blog is not an easy feat, and you will need to put in a lot of effort. Here are different income streams that you can consider making money from.

- Advertising: This is where most of the bloggers usually start. This is similar to the advertisements that you would find in magazines and newspapers. Once the web traffic to your blog starts growing, you can find advertisers who would be willing to pay you a fee to gain access to your followers. You will need to have decent traffic if you want to truly capitalize on this.

- Affiliate marketing: You can start earning by taking up some affiliate marketing on your blog. You simply have to post the affiliate links to specific products listed on a particular website. For instance, you have started a blog about baking recipes; you can perhaps post a link to a gourmet online store that you keep acquiring your produce from. By doing this, you will earn a commission on a sale that is made whenever a buyer clicks on the affiliate link.

- Events: This isn't something that a lot of bloggers tend to do, but it is quite lucrative as well. You can host an event and earn some money. You can host online or offline events, depending on your convenience. You can charge your readers for entering the contest or the event, or you can find a sponsor for the event. Online events have become quite popular these days.

- Recurring income: An increasing number of bloggers are opting for recurring income streams these days like membership or continuity programs. This is when the readers are required to pay a recurring fee to access premium content, some specific service, or online tools being offered on the blog.

- Promoting a business: You can start promoting regular brick-and-mortar businesses on your blogs. The businesses would pay you a fee for accessing your reader base.

- Services: You can also start offering different services to your readers like coaching, consulting, copywriting, training, designing, and much more.

While blogging, keep these simple things in mind.

You cannot post links directly on your blog. You will have to direct your users towards a homepage where the necessary content is present or the brand's website description that has a clickable link to it. A picture is indeed worth a thousand words. However, a collage that consists of 44 images isn't worth 4000 words. If you want to market your brand or business successfully, then make sure that the images you are posting are clear, identifiable, and large. Keep things simple. Make sure that you are posting actively and according to the engagement pattern of your followers. When it seems that they are most likely to engage, that's when you should post. This will take a while to get it right and spend some time trying to figure this out. It might not sound important, but it most certainly is. Keywords are quite important. Keywords help the users in discovering your content. Be judicious in your use of keywords and keyword phrases. Always remember to respond to any direct comments, opinions, and questions.

Chapter Nine: Vlogging

Vlogging refers to video blogging and in this vloggers share their ideas, thoughts, routines, snippets from their daily life and much more. A vlogger documents their daily life and shares the same on the Internet. This is done to gain the attention of the audience and to keep them engaged.

Here are a couple of things that you would need as a vlogger if you were interested in making money from vlogs.

The number of opportunities that come along your way will increase with an increase in the viewers your vlog receives. One of the most popular platforms for vlogging is YouTube. If you have a YouTube channel with a significant number of followers, then the number of opportunities you have will increase as well. You should be consistent with the way you upload your vlogs and engage with your viewers; growth is bound to happen. When you are consistent, people will automatically start liking and commenting on the vlogs you post. The greater the number of subscribers and followers you have, the higher are your chances of landing promotional gigs.

The cinematography does make a difference in profiting with vlogging. Essentially vlogging is about being innovative and being genuine on the camera. Notwithstanding that, what attracts a lot of people is great quality video. An excellent quality video implies your recordings must be splendidly shot, cinematography ought to be innovative, and the substance being shared is significant.

The narrating is likely the most critical piece of the vlog. If you want to get your audience hooked on to what you are offering, then the narrative needs to be engaging. It reflects in your entire vlog. It's something that associates a considerable measure of things together, for example, vlog story + vlog title + vlog thumbnail + vlog content. Each vlogger has an alternate method of recounting the story. Some of them have long and loquacious vlogs. They share their day to day life minutes while doing day by day routine errands, spending some time with their family while cooking, feasting at the lodging, and now and then shopping with family.

One of the essential things is an incredible thought process. It relies on the vlogger. What you are sharing should be a reflection of who you are. Vlogging is about inventiveness and also innovativeness. Try not to constrain yourself to a couple of thoughts that somebody tells you for profiting from vlogging. Continue researching and finding new ways to serve your crowd when you get started. After this point, consider benefiting because toward the day's end, any individual who ever profits with vlogging is somebody who began vlogging for enthusiasm and not to profit out of it.

You can just begin profiting with vlogging by joining the YouTube partner program. This is the least complex approach to begin. Ensure your record is in a great standing. Go to your dashboard and search for the adaptation tab to initiate it and follow simple steps to get started. When it's set, it may take a couple of days to get the endorsement, but once that is done, you'll be ready. From that point on, you'll be profiting off of your recordings.

Take up vlogging only if you are fascinated and passionate about it. You cannot fake enthusiasm, and you indeed cannot hold an audience if you don't like what you are doing. You can make use of your vlog to promote any particular product if you want to. If you have developed an affiliate marketing or selling the program for yourself, then you can certainly make use of your vlog for promoting the same. If you can hold onto your viewers and keep increasing the number of followers you have, then you are a step closer to obtaining sponsorships for yourself. You may have seen your most loved YouTubers discussing the products or the merchandise they offer through their online stores, and clearly, all the activity gets through their YouTube channels. Not just your merchandise, but you can make use of the same strategy for promoting any affiliate products as well. This is a good strategy for affiliate marketing and selling.

Chapter Ten:

Virtual Assistant

A virtual assistant is essentially a freelancer who provides online assistance by working remotely. You don't have to be physically present at the client's office anymore. You can work from home if you decide to become a virtual assistant. There is a lot of work that needs to be done in any business. However, not all are capable of hiring a person for every task. Most of the startups don't have the finances to hire full-time employees. In such a situation, they outsource a portion of their work to virtual assistants. There are different things that a virtual assistant can and will be required to do. In this chapter, I have categorized all the tasks that a virtual assistant will have to do into seven categories. You can work as a virtual assistant through websites such as fiverr.com and upwork.com.

General or administrative virtual assistants

They are like regular office secretaries. You need to have good time management skills and a good command over the language as well. The usual tasks that you might have to handle would be the emails of your boss and those of the clients, any telephonic inquiries, booking of appointments, managing the appointments, and database management.

Digital marketing virtual assistants

Usually, handles the online marketing campaigns of companies. Digital marketing virtual assistants can be categorized into social media management assistants, SEO assistants and content marketing assistants. The job description usually comprises of analyzing data to achieve the necessary return on investment, planning, scheduling and managing content, making a campaign strategy and analyzing its success, and conducting various analysis as well.

Programming virtual assistants

You will be hired as an assistant developer for a website or a mobile application. Your job profile would include the tasks of designing websites, applications, maintenance and updating the same, debugging and troubleshooting, and uploading new content regularly.

Design virtual assistants

As a design assistant, you will have to make the company's website easy to use and you should possess excellent graphic design skills. You might be required to design the business website, design the mobile application, flyers, business cards, promotional material, product shots, and infographic designs for the same.

Writing virtual assistants

You will be responsible for different types of content writing jobs. You can be a data entry clerk also at times. So, make sure that you are thoroughly enquiring about the position that you are applying for before taking up a job. Usually, you would be required to make plans for content, SEO researching, editing, proofreading, and writing content for SEO.

A/V editing virtual assistants

You will be responsible for all the background tasks that need to be done for editing audio and video. This could mean the removal of clutter, adding sounds for engaging the audience, adding any CGI, providing a sequence to the content given, and making the content audible and visible to the audience.

Financial virtual assistants

A financial virtual assistant would assist in documenting all the financial records, auditing financial statements, analyzing the given information, checking for any discrepancies, advising about money matters, and so on.

No professional degree is necessary to become a virtual assistant, but you should be familiar with the kind of job you are applying for. However, having experience in the area that you applied for will undoubtedly come in handy.

Chapter Eleven:
Freelance Writer/Transcriber

Do you like writing? Do you want to become a professional writer? If yes, then you can do that now! I am not saying that it is easy to become a professional writer, but at some point, you will have to sit down and write some original content. There are different ways in which you can get paid for your writing. Becoming a freelance writer is a great idea! In this chapter, you will learn about different ways in which you can turn your passion and flair for writing into an opportunity to earn money.

Starting a blog

If you want to become a writer, make sure that you have your blog. This will help you in developing a particular writing style as well as an audience for the same. You can advertise about yourself on your blog. Include a "hire me" link in your blog, so that the readers know that you are a writer for hire.

Pitching a guest post

You probably have a couple of blogs that you read daily. Why don't you consider pitching those bloggers to do a guest post on your blog? You can also think about collaborating with other bloggers who share similar interests. This helps in interacting with a broader audience. A lot of blogs also accept guest posts, and they will pay for the same as well. You will have to do a lot of research about this.

Your alma mater

Your alumni magazine probably needs writers, and they would probably love to hire their former students. Read through the guidelines, get acquainted with a few issues, and you can make a pitch for a great idea. Not just that, you can always look for other opportunities at your alma mater like drafting the regular notices and newsletters.

Writing a listicle

Who are the top 10 super villains in the Marvel universe? You are probably coming up with different names in your head. So, why don't you make a note of these names? There are different websites like Listverse or TonTenz that pay for witty and smart top 10 lists. Think about this option if you can come up with quirky ideas.

Self-publishing a book

If you like writing and you want to become an author, you no longer have to find a publisher for yourself. You can publish your book on Amazon or an eBook on Amazon Kindle Direct Publishing. You have to upload your book, get it ready for a kindle, and then start publicizing about it. Don't forget to mention this on your blog. If you aren't sure about finishing a novel, then you can think about serializing it.

Signing up for a content site

You can sign up with a content site and start writing content that you will get paid for. Get familiar with AP writing Style. Learn as much as you can about different styles of writing and make sure that you can follow the brief that a client gives.

Becoming a copywriter

Once you know how to write good content for content sites, you can think about becoming a copywriter as well. You can look at the listings posted on different websites for hiring copywriters, and you can get started with it right away.

Writing fan-fiction

Did you know that Amazon Kindle Worlds is going to pay you to write licensed fan fiction about top-rated television shows? Well, yes! You can certainly cash in on this opportunity. You will need to write 10000+ words on a character you adore, and you will get paid for doing the same.

A good grip on the language and an effortless style of writing are all that you need for becoming a good content writer.

Chapter Twelve:

Amazon FBA

What is FBA?

Fulfillment by Amazon is popularly known as FBA, and it is a third-party logistics service started by Amazon. It helps millions of sellers registered with Amazon across the globe to fulfill their orders. FBA provides you with the option of shipping your old as well as new products to Amazon, instead of shipping them directly to your customers. Once your products reach the Amazon Fulfillment Centers, they will handle the rest. When orders are placed for your products, Amazon will directly pick the stock up from these fulfillment centers and ship them to the customers. They will provide you with shipping facilities, customer service once the order is delivered, and manage customer returns. This will help you save a significant amount of time, effort, and money. Many sellers who have opted for FBA have ended up saving approximately 50% of their shipping costs.

Working with FBA

The working of FBA can be summed up in one sentence "you sell it, we ship it." A private label seller should make the most of Amazon's fulfillment network and their expertise to help in the growth of their business. Your listings on Amazon.com can make use of the free shipping services offered by Amazon, provided the bill amount is above a specified value.

The FBA listings on Amazon.com are listed and then sorted according to the price, and there are no shipping costs involved if the combined value of products is above the value of $35. The FBA listings when accompanied by the FBA logo lets the customers know that the shipping, packing, customer service and all returns are handled solely by Amazon. Using the inventory stored at the Amazon fulfillment center can complete fulfillment of orders, even from other sales channels. The online user interface will let you manage your inventory and at the same time will provide the necessary direction so that the inventory can be returned at any time.

FBA in motion

The following steps explain in brief how the process of FBA works:

Sending products to Amazon

You can send your products, new and used to Amazon's fulfillment center. Seller Central-

Upload the details of your listings. You can decide whether you want Amazon to fulfill either partly or in whole your inventory or not. You can use FBA's Label Service to print labels, or you can also make use of PDF Labels that are provided by Amazon. You can either select your carrier, or you can make use of Amazon's discounted shipping facility.

Receipt and storing of goods by Amazon

As soon as Amazon receives the products, it scans the inventory. The unit dimensions for storage are recorded. Using Amazon's integrated tracking system can monitor your inventory. The products received are cataloged and stored.

Requests for orders

Amazon fulfills the orders placed regardless of whether it has been placed on Amazon.com or any other fulfillment request has been sent for sales, not on Amazon.

Products are picked and packed

Web-to-warehouse, sorting system and high-speed picking system are the technologies adopted by Amazon that let it locate the desired products. Customers have the option of combining products.

Shipping of products

The products are shipped to the customers through the Amazon's fulfillment centers. The products are shipped to the customer depending upon the method selected by them. The required tracking information of the products dispatched is sent to the customers. Customer service can always be contacted for orders that are placed on Amazon.com.

Here are some simple steps that you can follow to add Fulfillment by Amazon to your selling on Amazon Account:

- Go to the Inventory option and click on Manage Inventory.

- To select a product that you want to include in the FBA listing, just click on the box next to it in the left column.

- Now go to Actions and click on Changed to Fulfilled by Amazon.

- And then, all you need to do is follow the directions given to create your first shipment.

Things needed

A Smartphone

A Smartphone is a multidisciplinary tool that finds use in almost all sectors. In the modern age, this tool has proved to be a necessity rather than a luxury. A computer with an active Internet connection is also useful. As your business develops, a Smartphone would be preferred as it gives you a greater sense of flexibility.

A scouting app

A scouting app is handy for a developing business, which can be easily installed on your Smartphone.

A printer

A good quality inkjet color printer with A4 paper sheets (11×17 inches long grain paper)

Packaging equipment

This is the main component of the toolkit. As a seller, you should never run out of these tools. Stack up on your cartons, boxes, labeling sheets, tapes and other stationery that you use for packaging your products.

Chapter Thirteen:

Sell Your Knowledge

Setting up a secondary line of income does sound tempting, doesn't it? However, not everyone has the time to start their own full-fledged business or even freelance. This doesn't mean that there aren't any opportunities for you out there. If you are knowledgeable about a specific area, you can come up with different ways in which you can make use of that knowledge of yours.

E-Book or a white paper

You can transform all the knowledge you possess and the experiences you have had as an investment! You will need to spend considerable time and energy to write an e-book or even publish a white paper, but it will be worth your while. Your vendor will take a cut, but apart from it, you can start selling your work almost immediately! You can write about anything that you are interested in. You can write how-to guides, recipe books, or even papers addressing any of the current issues.

A seminar or a class

Seminars and classes are time-sensitive when compared to other projects that don't require any interaction with others. There are a lot of different ways in which you can make it flexible. One of the most basic things that you will have to do is select a time and date for the class that will work well with your schedule. Once you have done this, you can start planning other details for your class. The primary challenge with this idea is that you will need to be able to convince prospective students to enroll in your class. So, you will need to be able to market your skills well.

Tutoring

If you are good at a particular subject or topic that is taught in school- from kindergarten to grad school- you can consider tutoring. You don't have to worry about any geographical barriers. You can set up your online tutoring program. This will allow you to work with students who are situated in different time zones as well.

Writing for websites

There are plenty of websites that allow writers to write and post numerous articles on their websites. The website is entitled to a percentage of the profits you earn. You can write about anything that interests you, and there are no restrictions regarding any deadlines. You can even stop writing whenever you feel like.

Consulting services

Have you heard of consulting services? Well, with the advent of the Internet, you can offer these services online as well! You can enlist yourself on a website that will help in connecting you with prospective clients who are looking for services that you offer.

Answering questions

Various websites offer payment for answering specific questions. Depending on your areas of interest, you can undoubtedly find a site that you can make use of. If you have good business acumen or a degree in law, you can make use of this to answer specific questions that fall within the purview of your area of expertise.

Chapter Fourteen:

Niche Stores on eBay, Shopify

If you want to become a successful seller, then you should think about niche marketing and selling. You should consider about starting your niche store. A niche is a small part or the sub-market of a more extensive market. Niche stores are usually very competitive, and they have a right demand for the product they are selling.

Find a niche

You will need to find a niche that suits you and the requirements you have in mind. When you do find a niche that you like, type the same into the search bar that's provided on eBay. This will help you in checking the competition that exists. Since you are just getting started with niche selling, make sure that there isn't too much competition. If not, you will have a tough time while selling. Consider different sub-categories of niches as well. Even if it sounds eccentric, it might be lucrative. Do a lot of research and don't just stick to the most obvious options that are available online.

Select a product

You will need to select a product that you want to sell! eBay and Shopify have numerous sellers listed on it. Select products you have a passion for and the work will come easy; you'll enjoy building your shop. Opening up your niche shop can be fun and is an excellent idea if you were always interested in starting your own business.

Your competition

Make it difficult for your competition to offer the same type of products that you are offering. Or make your pricing strategy quite attractive. You should have a unique selling point that will distinguish you from all the other sellers within your niche. Also, make sure that the market is large enough for you to survive.

Setting up your store

You will need to create an eye-catching storefront. There are many ways in which you can personalize your storefront. This personalization is of great importance to ensure that your store stands apart from the rest so that you can grab the attention of potential customers and promote your brand. You can add a banner to your storefront. A banner is a graphic that would run across the page of your store, and you can create this without much difficulty by making use of graphics software and programs like Picasa, Photoshop, and Windows Paint and so on. Always include a shop title and shop announcement. Your shop title would be similar to a tagline, and it would sum up in brief what your shop is all about. Shop announcement is different from a shop title; this would be appearing on the banner, providing information about the products you sell, the materials used and your artistic philosophy if any exists. Your shop announcement can also be made use of to broadcast about any upcoming. There are different types of items that you might sell. If you are selling products like notebooks, magnets, pens, picture frames, then you can organize this as stationery. You can make use of further sections like size, type, material or price as filters when selling these.

Pricing your product

When you start selling your products or goods on your eBay or Shopify store, you might wonder the amount you should charge the customers for your items. If you want to have a profitable online store on these platforms, then you will need to be comfortable going over some numbers and doing a little math regarding your pricing strategy.

There are two simple formulae that you will need to learn for this, and they aren't difficult.

The first one is;

(Materials+Labor+Overhead) x2 = Wholesale price

and the second one is;

Wholesale price x2 = Retail price.

But the cost of shipping isn't included in this. The second formula can be adjusted according to your convenience. When you multiply the wholesale price by 2, it will provide the retail price. At times the sellers opt for a number higher than two like 2.5 or 3 to determine their retail price, provided that the market is willing to bear such an expense.

Compose product photos

Products photos that are well photographed can act as a catalyst to promote sales for your eBay store, but you needn't hire a professional photographer to do this. You can very well compose your photos, here are some pointers that will help you portray your product in the best possible manner. All you need is a little bit of artistic flair, some patience, and the following guidelines. You should angle your camera; this means that tilting the camera a little so that it would put the subject matter slightly off center and create some movement and flow. This would produce a picture that is more intriguing. Make sure that you fill the frame with your product so that it not only seems more appealing, but the potential buyers can also see how well-crafted your product is. To highlight your piece dramatically and adding a little bit of panache to it, you can blur the background so that the focus automatically shifts to your product. Always frame your picture with a darker element. You can group your products together, especially if you are into designing or creating itsy bitsy products, then to attract attention, you can group several products together so that the buyer can see how cohesive your products are together. Make use of the rule of thirds. This is a straightforward rule; you will need to divide the scene that you are photographing into nine parts by making use of two horizontal and vertical lines like a tic tac toe grid. This will help in piquing the interest of the viewer.

Compose titles

An item title would be similar to a good headline for a product, and it needs to be designed in such a manner that it would grab the buyer's attention and get them to want to read more about that particular item. You will need to keep it short and contain it to within 155 characters inclusive of spaces. Describe the items at the beginning of the item title so that it would help in improving the chances of searching for a specific item.

Chapter Fifteen:

Direct Sales - What it takes

The process of marketing as well as selling products, in a non-retail setup, directly to the consumer is referred to as direct selling. The sales take place at work, home, or even at a location apart from a store. This system helps in the elimination of middlemen involved in the distribution network. Instead, the products go from the manufacturer to the company taking up direct selling, to the rep or the distributor, and then to the consumer. The products that are sold through direct selling are not usually found in retail outlets. This means that the only way to acquire them is the distributor or the reps. Direct selling isn't the same as direct marketing. In direct marketing, the company bypasses the distributors and other mediators, and instead directly markets to the consumer. Have you ever heard of companies like Silpada or Avon? These are direct selling companies. Direct selling offers you the convenience of working at your hours, earning bonuses, and trips too! You will need to pay a small fee to acquire the starter kit and to make a commission from all the sales you finalize. If you are interested in becoming a successful rep, then here are a couple of things that you should keep in mind.

Company strategy

Some companies will charge you about $10 to buy a starter kit, while for others you might need to stock up on more inventory, and then there are those that have a strict deadline as well. The chances of your success are quite high if your personality and your selling style go hand in hand with the company strategy. So, do some research and talk to a company recruiter about the monthly quota, any incentives, and the selling tools that are necessary.

A product that excites you

You can do your best if you believe in the product that you are selling. If the product that you are selling excites you, it is very likely that the same energy would be transferred to the consumer as well. For instance, if you are a sales rep for a company that deals in clothing and jewelry, then you are the model for the products you are trying to sell! If the thought of maintaining manicured nails for showing off a cocktail ring sounds too time-consuming for you, then this isn't for you. So, select a product that genuinely excites you.

Attitude matters

You must set a couple of realistic goals for yourself regarding what you would like to earn. Like with anything else in life, there will be times when you will feel discouraged. Therefore, you need to set goals for yourself and make sure that the goals are attainable.

Good at networking

Direct selling is all about attracting clients and closing a sale. If you are a social butterfly, then this option might be quite useful! You obviously cannot rely solely on your friends and family members. You should be able to socialize and talk to potential customers at any time and any place without any hesitation.

There are a couple of things that you should keep in mind while you are thinking about making money by taking up direct selling. There are legitimate companies, and then there are those companies that are trying to scam you. Here are a couple of suspicious things that you should watch out for.

The startup cost is high. You have to buy a lot of inventory that cannot be returned. Profits are based on recruiting others, and there isn't any proper information about the company or the firm.

Introduction to Internet Marketing

Internet marketing is imperative to your business. It will help you align your business with the many ways people decide to buy things. Studies performed by companies like Gartner show there are more people who use social media and do their research on mobile apps to carry out the price and product research before making a decision. Internet marketing gives you the chance to build relationships with your existing customers and find new customers with low-cost, regular personalized communications. If you're still not convinced, here are six reasons why internet marketing is important.

Convenience – internet marketing gives you the chance to be open for business all the time without worrying about opening an actual store and paying overtime. Offering products on the internet makes it more convenient for your customers. They can browse the store online and then place an order when it is the most convenient for them.

Reach – when you market on the internet you can overcome distance barriers. You can sell your products anywhere in the country without having to open an actual store, which widens your target market. You can also build a business that can export goods without the need of numerous distributors in other countries. However, if you do choose to sell internationally, you need to use local services to know if your product will sell well with the locals and comply with city and county regulations. Localization services will let you know if you need to modify any products to show the local market and helps with translation.

Cost – internet marketing tends to cost less than marketing through physical outlets. You won't have recurring costs that come up, and you don't have to worry about any maintenance.

Personalization – you can personalize specific offers to your customers through internet marketing by keeping a profile of what they buy regularly and history. By tracking product information and web pages that prospects visit, you will be able to make targeted offers. The information you get from tracking their website visits also provides information to help with cross-selling campaigns so you can increase sales value.

Relationships – the internet gives you a great platform to build relationships with your customers and helps you keep your customer base. Once a customer has bought products from you, you can build a relationship by sending them an email that confirms the transaction. Emailing your customers with offers that are just for them helps to keep the relationship. You can also ask them to provide product reviews.

Social – internet marketing gives you the chance to be a part of the growing power of social media. Harvard Business School published an article that highlighted the link between social media and growing online revenue. According to their research, consumers responded stronger to the social network influence, which increased sales of around 5%. Take advantage of this influence by using social media as a tool to help with internet marketing.

Impact of Social Media

With social media marketing, businesses reported a 100% higher lead-to-close rate than any other market. Around 84% of all B2B marketers use social media in some way. No matter your market or product, making use of social media as a marketing tool will help you expand your brand.

At this point, not being active on social media is like having a flip phone out during a business meeting, and then complaining about the fact that your boss keeps giving somebody else all the good jobs.

Yet there are still people with flip phones, and some still buck the system and say, what is marketing through social media going to help me do? Do I have to have it? Yes. Here are some very compelling reasons why.

1. Social media helps to drive targeted traffic

Taking an amazing selfie and creating a new page on your website is pretty much the same thing. You want everybody around the world to see it, but you're not interested in begging for the attention, even worse, pay somebody for it. This is the reason why for landing pages and selfies, having social posts that are well placed makes the biggest difference. One link shared on Reddit has been able to bring more than 20,000 visitors in a single link. Websites shared to StumbleUpon can up a page from a handful of visitors to hundreds.

2. Social media helps to boost your SEO

People who constantly use search engines know the pages that are always earning traffic and which are ignored and forgotten. A great SEO content strategy is a crucial part of getting the best spots in search engine rankings, but they will climb faster by driving traffic to your optimized pages. You can successfully drive traffic to your website or blog by utilizing social media platforms.

3. Social media can build real relationships

Part of what makes Instagram and Twitter marketing so amazing is that fact that you can so easily communicate with your customers. You can look at their updates and tweets to get information about their life. What products do they buy? What are their plans for the weekend? What posts do they like to share?

4. Users are responsive to your messages

Facebook and Twitter are viewed as social networks by most people and not tools for marketing. As a result, they won't view your posts as advertisements thus making them more open to hearing what you want to share with them. This will then turn into more web traffic when you share your link in your posts.

5. Social Media ads allow targeting and retargeting

The customizable nature of social media ads is what makes it so important. You can target certain users with Facebook ads through things like certain location, industry, purchase history, education level, and pages they've liked.

6. Problems get immediate response

If a problem with your service or product were to come up, then you will want to know about it as soon as possible. With the feedback that you will receive through social media, you will know when any issues come up.

7. Builds brand loyalty

Texas Tech University discovered that brands that had social media accounts had a larger number of loyal customers. You can easily see why: when you interact and engage with social media, they start to see you less as a corporation and more as a like-minded person or group of people.

8. The competition is social, so you should be too

91% of businesses will have more than a single social media account. This isn't a good thing to fall behind your competition on because it's going to be extremely hard to play catch up. When you're active and engaging on several networks, you will be able to gain followers and friends first, and the competition will have to play catch up.

9. Social media will get you more sales

70% of business-to-consumer marketers get their customers through Facebook, and 84% of VPs and CEOs say they use social media to make purchasing decisions.

10. It's free

You can't really argue with that logic, can you? If you control your own accounts, running social networking is about as cheap as it comes. If you hire an online PR agency or social media management, it will run you about $3000 to $7000 each month, but it will probably be an investment that you will see a return on. On a smaller scale, you can hire a virtual assistant to manage your social media. You can hire a virtual assistant on websites such as Freelancer.com or Upwork.com at fairly inexpensive rates.

Facebook

Facebook is the top social platform for businesses to use. 41% of US small businesses make use of Facebook in the marketing strategy. While it's a great marketing tool, you have to understand the best practices and strategies to see the most return.

1. Optimize your Facebook page of likes and SEO

Your page is where your marketing efforts start. Ideally, you want it to rank in Google and Facebook search so that customers can easily find you. Once they have found you, it should be appealing so people will like you.

Pick a memorable and descriptive username – Your Facebook page username is the web address for your page. As a default, you will be given a random URL made up of numbers. The username needs to convey your pages topic or your full business name accurately. You will need 25 likes to customize your vanity URL.

Descriptive keywords should be used in the About section – The About section is the main text-based real estate on a Facebook page. Make sure you use accurate, descriptive words for your products and business. Use keywords customers may use when searching for you. Adding your website URL in the description will encourage clicks to your site.

Use the appropriate category – Too often businesses choose the wrong category. This is a problem, especially if you want your page to be in the Facebook Graph Search. If you are a local business, make sure you select that as you type because this will ensure people can "check-in" at your business. If you don't have actual walk-in traffic and don't have an actual need for check-ins, picking 'Companies & Organizations' would be more appropriate.

Optimize images – Your profile and cover photos are what people see first. Your images need to be professional quality, and accurately reflect the feel and look of your brand. Optimal sizes would be 851X315 pixels for your cover photo and 160X160 pixels for your profile photo.

Make use of pinned posts – Research has found the most people will only visit your page once. They will like it, and then interact with posts that appear on their newsfeed, but will rarely visit your wall. That means your main job is to get people to click like. Facebook lets admins pin one post on their page. The topic should be unique, interesting, and contain an eye-catching image.

2. Make use of Facebook groups to engage with your market

Pages may be the primary marketing tool on Facebook; groups can be an effective add-on in many niches and industries. Groups can lead to more traffic, increased engagement, and increased authority in your niche.

When you participate in other's industry-related groups, you will be able to establish yourself as an authority in your niche. When you offer useful advice and tips, you become a valued group member. As people grow to trust you, they will want to learn more about you.

The most beneficial part of groups is to participate and create your own interest-related group. They give you the change to engage with your audience in a more personal way, and it allows you to become a part of your customer's day-to-day conversations.

3. Encourage share with Facebook Plugins and Buttons

Your Facebook page and website need to work seamlessly together. Your marketing funnel will probably work by moving Facebook traffic to your blog or website. You should also make sure that your website visitors will have a way to share and like your Facebook content.

Make sure that each piece of your content has a share and like button next to it. This can be added manually or with the use of a third party service such as WordPress or Add This plugin.

To allow your website visitors the chance interact with and like your page, install the page plugin to your site's sidebar. When you set up the plugin, it will give you options regarding how you want it to look. It's best if you choose 'Show Page Posts' so that your website visitors can preview the type of content you normally share.

4. Get your posts seen by more fans

A big complaint amongst page owners is many of their fans don't see their posts. Facebook stated that the reason for the falling reach is the result of two things: One, the sheer amount of content that is shared every day doesn't allow enough space in user's newsfeed. This makes placement a fierce competition.

The second reason is that Facebook shows the most relevant content to its users. They determine relevancy through how a person has interacted with a page, the type of post, and the page's popularity among all users. This means that the more popular your posts are, the more often they will be in your fan's feeds.

Here are some strategies to help up your chances of showing up in your fan's feeds:

- Make use of videos – research has shown that videos lead in terms of organic reach.
- Check your page insights to see the types of content that are resonating – the insights page contains a wealth of data as to what content is getting the most engagement from your audience. See the types of posts that get the most traction, as well as what your audience is passionate about.
- With promotional content, make sure to include an engaging backstory

Make sure you add plenty of engaging content to your promotional posts to make sure that it is seen.

5. How often and when to post

There are lots of business owners that get hung up on posting the perfect time, but the truth is, there isn't a one-size-fits-all approach to posting. All of the research has been done to find the optimal posting time and frequency, but this should be used as a starting point for your own research. Check your own Facebook Insights to see when your audience views posts.

Some research has found the posting on Thursdays and Friday's results in better engagement. The best posting times seem to vary, but 1 pm and 3 pm seem to be the best place to start testing.

When it comes to frequency, try to find a balance between informative and annoying. There are some businesses that do well posting five to ten times every day. For some, once a day or three times a week is appropriate. A good rule of thumb is five to ten posts a week. If you post less than two posts a week, you keep your audience engaged.

6. Paid options to increase reach and likes

While you can get a good reach through free strategies, you may want to also supplement organic strategies with paid choices.

Post boosts – when you boost a post it will increase its visibility in newsfeeds. You can choose to have the post shown to fans, fans friends, or others that you pick through targeting. This is a quick and easy way to expand the reach of your posts, but promoting your posts can be better.

Promoted posts – you can get to promoted posts through your Facebook Ads Manager. Head to the Facebook Ad Creator and click on boost your posts. This may still be called boosting; you will see more targeting and budgeting options than just clicking on a boost from your page.

7. When to promote

A hard decision you will have to make is picking the best time to promote a post. You should only promote a post that helps you to meet a specific goal, such as driving website traffic or selling something. Once you've decided to promote a post, I suggest using Jay Behr's STIR strategy. The best practice is to ask yourself a series of questions about S – shelf-life, T – timing, I – impact, R – results of a paid post.

8. Facebook Ads

Unfortunately, it's extremely easy to send out a lot of money on your ads without achieving your desired goal. Ads can be a helpful way to get conversions, traffic, and likes, but there are some practices you need to follow.

Use audience targeting – if you advertise to a general audience, you will be throwing away money. You should also test out a variety of targeting options because they tend to effective options.

Most important content first – users normally see content near the beginning of your ad. Because of this, you need to put your most important content, such as a call to action, such as "buy now", near the beginning.

Rotate ads every one to two weeks – this is especially true if you use specific targeting. You should change up your ad's copy and image every week or so. If you keep the same content, you are decreasing your chance of getting your ad noticed.

A strong call to action – always tell your users what you want them to do. While you don't have to tell them to click your ad specifically, you should tell them why they should click on it. Give them a compelling reason why they can't live without it.

Twitter

As of 2017, Twitter has an average of 330 million monthly active users. That's a lot of people that you could market to if you know how to. So what is the best way to leverage the 140-character social network to help you drive traffic to your website or business? Let's look at 14 ways to optimize your Twitter marketing.

1. Optimize your bio

You have to make sure that your company has a well-branded voice and identity. This means you need to have a bio that lets your visitors know who you are and make sure that you include a link to your landing page or website. It's important that you keep your tone consistent on everything so that people can get a sense of who you are.

2. Find the experts and influencers in your same target and engage with them on a regular basis

Make use of Twitter as a search tool to locate like-minded influencers, prospects, and customers by looking up keywords related to your niche. Follow them and interact with them daily. Create a list of the most influential people that are a part of your niche. This can include potential partners, writers, big-name bloggers, potential customers or clients, leaders, journalists, and so on. Make a private Twitter list and add them. Try to engage with them every day. Make sure you keep interactions casual and helpful. Don't sound promotional.

3. Involved colleagues

If you have more than one person in your business, then your first step is to build your brand through internal means. Make sure everybody that works with you follows you on Twitter and that they tweet, retweet, and engage with your content.

4. Tweet regularly

Regular tweets show people that you are a healthy and active profile. If you only tweet once a week or month, then people will end up forgetting about you. Daily posts and engagement are best so that you stay in your follower's mind. Make sure your content is useful and relevant.

5. Ask people for some Twitter love

Don't be afraid to ask your followers to retweet, favorite or mention your tweets, or to add your content to a fresh tweet on their page.

6. Track and respond to mentions

Keep track of your brand keywords and mentions so that you know what others are saying. Make sure that you respond politely if appropriate. Monitor their conversations and jump in at an appropriate time.

7. Retweet

Make sure that you make use of retweets. This will help to link you with leadership within your niche.

8. Favorite tweets

A lot of people don't realize that they can have favorite tweets, but it can be useful in getting someone's attention more so than a mention or a retweet.

9. Follow hashtags or trends

Take a look at what hashtags are trending and topics and figure out a way to connect them to your brand. When you can put your business within the group of trending topics, people will see your handle whenever they search for those trending hashtags. You should make sure that you use hashtags sparingly. They can easily become seen as Twitter spam when you attach them to irrelevant contents or overuse them.

10. Offer special deals or discounts to your followers

Run contests on Twitter like "The next 50 people that retweet one of my posts will get a 50 percent off coupon." You can have people post pictures of themselves using your product.

11. Use videos and images

Videos and photos can drive three to four more clicks on Twitter. Rich content has been proven to get a lot more shares and clicks than plain text tweets.

12. Use promoted tweets

Directly target your audience by using promoted tweets. If you fail to clearly state who it is you want to reach, it could end up costing you money and time. Your goal is to provide value that makes you look credible, not like you're trying to trick people into clicking your link.

13. Integrate Twitter with all your marketing efforts

Twitter is more effective when you use them along with your other marketing work. If you choose to run a contest or promotion on Twitter, let your email subscribers know about it, as they are also still an important part of your customer base. You can also periodically tweet out your mailing list link; this will allow you to tap your Twitter followers into your email list.

14. Make use of Twitter analytics

Make use of Twitter's analytics each day to help you understand what is working for your audience that you have built. When you're in the analytics dashboard, you will be able to figure out when your best days to share a tweet are, the kind of content that gets more likes, and your follower's demographics. Replicate what is working for you.

Instagram

It's definitely not a secret that a business needs to have a presence on Instagram. Instagram has more than 500 million users making is a network that provides an amazing platform for marketing to reach customers all over the world.

You will have to increase your following on a consistent and steady basis to improve your Instagram marketing. After all, the more followers that are in contact with you on Instagram, the bigger the audience you have to reach with each of your posts.

1. Make use of free Instagram tools

Instagram has implemented a business profile that resembles Facebook's business profiles, complete with a "contact" call-to-action that allows followers to text, email, or call your business.

Besides the contact button, businesses also have analytics, or Insights, that gives users a way to check their engagement and impression date. If you are interested in getting your business started with Instagram, then it is in your best interest to convert your personal account to a business account so that you can take advantage of all of their options. The better you can understand the ways that your followers interact with your content, the easier it will be to make improvements to your engagement.

2. Cross promotion

If you want to easily add followers on Instagram that are already a fan of your brand, then you should post on all of your accounts. Invite followers on Twitter or Facebook to follower you on Instagram. They already follow you, so they are interested in what your brand has to offer, so this will provide them with a different way to connect with you.

You should never assume that all of your posts reach all of the followers connected with you. A lot of people will start to move away from different platforms, and some are more active on one than they are on another. This is why you want your followers connected to as many of your social accounts as possible.

3. Don't overwhelm them

You should post often enough that you stay relevant, but not so much that you start to overwhelm your followers. This will only end up causing them to unfollow you because they feel as if you are always in their face.

There are no magic posting formulas that work for everybody. You will have to do your own tests to see how your followers respond. A good starting point is to post two posts a day and alternate the times to find out when you get the most engagement. Then you can begin to experiment with more or fewer posts each day. Make sure you pay close attention to engagement. Once you figure out your sweet spot, the testing isn't really going to stop, as the number of followers grows, you will have to make adjusts.

4. Interact with your followers

If somebody spends time leaving a comment on a post, take a couple of seconds to reply back and thank them. Just that bit of engagement can create a loyal follower, and it will also promote your brand.

Also, try incorporating things into your posts to interact with your followers. Something as simple as, "tag four friends that would love this," can expand your brand to a bigger audience, and it will provide you with new followers. Since a friend is introducing them to your profile, they are less resistance, which will result in most of the people who were tagged to follow you.

5. Make a hashtag

Coming up with an interactive hashtag is the perfect way to increase your engagement, you just need to make sure that you are correctly using those hashtags. A great way to use hashtags is to create a hashtag that customers use when they post pictures of themselves with your products.

6. Repurpose relevant content from other users

If you are finding it difficult to create enough relevant content to meet the needs of your follower's, consider repurposing the content from somebody else's Instagram. You need to make sure that you give them credit for tagging and mentioning them.

7. Use creativity to connect with your followers

When you are creative with your images, it helps you to connect with your followers. This is a more effective tactic than posting images that only look like an advertisement.

YouTube

YouTube is one of the top two search engines in the world, streaming videos to a population of people that exceed the amount of people in Indonesia, the US, and Brazil combined. With more than 100 hours of videos being added every single minute and 6 billion hours of videos being watched each month, it's definitely an amazing marketing tool that you need to take advantage of. So what is the best way to get this massive audience to get to know your business? Let's look at some tips that will help you bring in the followers.

1. Create a channel that shows what your brand is about

YouTube provides you with the chance to include your company's voice with tools that let you add logos, create a color scheme, and use custom tags. There are plenty of popular YouTube pages to view to see good examples of this; PBS is a great one to check out.

2. Make use of the right words

When somebody searches for videos, YouTube uses the keywords that you add to your video, so you want to ensure that you are as specific as possible when describing and naming your videos.

3. Add your other social profiles

You should treat your YouTube channel the same way that you treat a company website. Make sure that you include links to all of your other social media accounts.

4. Make a trailer

Come up with a two to three-minute video that helps to represent what your company is about. This gives you a chance to provide people a little glimpse into what your business is like.

5. Upload how-to videos about your service or product

People love to turn to the internet for their questions. If your service or product requires any explanation, demonstrate that through an informative video. This will also bring more traffic to your channel. If you have services and products that aren't all that complicated, you could make videos that incorporate new and fun ways to see your business. To help gain interest, an ad agency made a video that depicted a scene that people could relate to. They were able to get the attention of tens of thousands of viewers.

6. Get noticed

This is the biggest challenge for all videos. Getting the attention of billions of viewers that are searching through YouTube on any given day can be difficult. It helps to grab their attention by using an attention-grabbing image as your video's thumbnail.

7. Include testimonials

You need to establish your reputation and gain your viewers confidence by uploading testimonials you receive from customers that have used and bought your services or products. This will help potential customers to put any worries they may have to rest.

YouTube is a site that billions of people visit trying to discover new businesses like yours. Begin making use of this online resource for your business so that you can spend more time doing what you love.

Pinterest

If you believe that Twitter and Facebook are the only decent social marketing tools, then you need to think again.

Say hello to Pinterest. Pins on Pinterest are 100 times more shareable than a tweet is. On average a retweet hits only 1.4%. The half-life of a pin is 16000 times longer than a Facebook post.

Besides from its ability to feed obsessions with amazing exotic destination vacations and gorgeous foods, Pinterest's real powers are the features they provide business accounts. When you become a part of the 500,000 businesses with a Pinterest account, you will get the extra marketing features to help promote your business on a fast-growing and popular social media platform.

Creating a popular pin:

Social Media Examiner has described Pinterest as a visual search engine. Just like when you create a new article or post on Instagram, you have to make sure the content is searchable. If it can't be searched, then it won't be found or read.

The best categories – If you are educated about which categories fair well on Pinterest, then you will be able to get a better idea of what boards will work. The top ten most popular categories on Pinterest are food and drink, DIY crafts, home décor, women's fashion, other, weddings, design, hair and beauty, art, and kids. If there is no connection in your business with weddings or DIY crafts, then you shouldn't create a board for either one of the categories.

Working images – You can clearly see how visual Pinterest is. With such an emphasis on images, your images are the most important part of your pins. For a top pin, you have to have a clear, high-resolution image; these are more professional and appealing. Lighter colored images are repined 20 times more often than dark. Images that don't have faces are repinned 23% more often.

Optimal size – Every pin has to have the same width size, but their length is unlimited. The best size that you should go for is 736x1102 pixels.

Instructographics – Sometimes that unlimited length on Pinterest can come in handy. Pinterest coined the term instructographic and is pretty much the same thing as an infographic. These tend to be popular because of they are very DIY and how-to in nature, which just happens to be the second most popular category.

Getting your pins shared and seen:

Creating a fantastic pin is only part of the game. Getting your pin seen and shared is another story. Nobody will be able to locate your pin if you don't optimize if for engagement.

Posting time – Just like Facebook, Twitter, and Instagram, there are optimal times to post on Pinterest. The best time will depend on your followers, so you need to test to see what times work the best for you. For a good place to start, SocialFresh says that 8 pm and 1 am EST and 2 pm and 4 pm EST are the best posting times. HubSpot also stated that Saturday morning is THE best posting time.

Pin from your website – Place a Pin It button to the images on your website or phone app directly through Pinterest. This buttons will help to direct your website visitors to visit your Pinterest or to pin some of the content from your website to their account. If you don't use the buttons, then there isn't much chance that your site will have interaction with your Pinterest.

Connect your other accounts – It's not fun if you have to start over locating followers when you start a new social account. It's extremely easy to add your Facebook and Twitter accounts to a Pinterest account. This will help you to reach a larger amount of followers by tapping into your other social accounts that you are already established on. This helps you to share your content on several platforms, making your audience larger.

Share pins in a newsletter – Get rid of the difficulty of attracting new people to view your pins by sharing the pins with them. An email newsletter is a great way to add a couple of your most recent pins and to direct them to your account.

SEO – You have to make sure that you use SEO strategies to help your pins get discovered. Don't fret though, it won't take too much optimization for your pins. Make use of tools like Google AdWords Keyword Planner to figure out which related keywords are the most popular. Add these keywords to your pin titles and your pin descriptions. You can also add them to your pin image file name. Just like any other SEO optimization, make sure that you don't end up sounding too "keywordy." Don't over the top and add several keywords to your description and title and come off like a robot. Optimize you pin, but make sure that you still sound like a human.

Engagement to build followers and relationships:

After you can make good pins and get them seen, the next thing you need to do is to use your pins to make relationships with influencers and followers that will increase your reach. When you have more reach, you will create more success.

When you understand what other users are looking for when they follow different accounts, will ultimately help you to provide them the things they want. This will then grow your following.

In on Pinterest study, The University of Minnesota discovered that three biggest factors that Pinterest users take into consideration during their "should I follow" decision are:

- The amount of boards you have
- How many pins you have
- The number of accounts you are following and are following you

Post frequently – To grow your followers, you need to post between five to 30 new pins each day. You have to make sure that you aren't just repining things that other people have posted, but pinning unique content pins. A word of warning, don't post 30 pins within a five-minute time span. Spread out the post throughout the day. A good tip is to make a secret board. You can make all of you pins for that day and post them to the secret board, and then send them out at different times of the day.

Engage with your followers – As with Twitter, Facebook, and Instagram comment, you should engage with your followers directly by commenting back to them and answering their questions. Go the extra mile and use their names. This will bring your customer service to a new level.

Comment on other's pins – Engaging with people isn't a one-way street. You have to reach out to other follower's and their boards. Place comments on their pins so that they can feel more connected to you. It also helps that their followers will also see your brand.

Engage and follow with the most popular boards – You can learn a lot from people who have already struck gold with Pinterest. See what they pin, what boards they have, and how they engage. You want to reach their level. If you comment on their popular pins, you will be sharing your brand name with a large number of people.

Ask to join group boards. By doing this you gain their followers and grow your exposure. Most groups will be very receptive, especially if you have a lot of good content. When you go to the group board you will want to email the group's administrator whose profile will be the first circle on the top right, above the boards. Send them a friendly email asking to join their group.

Website Design Strategies

To name just a few, websites such as Wix.com, GoDaddy, and SiteBuilder.com are very user-friendly and intuitive when considering building your own website. Designing websites is not art. It does involve many different skills like art, layout, typography, and copywriting that are all stuck together to make an interface that uses features that are nice looking words but shows functionality and ease of access to the content it features.

To be able to combine all of these elements together and get results you need a clear direction. These directions should guide all aspects of the design to one common goal. You need to think strategically.

You are probably wondering what strategic design is. Strategic design happens when you fuse your goals with all aspects of the design process. You are not just designing an interface that is accessible, usable and looks good. You are designing one that will allow you to accomplish your objectives.

Many websites look great and incorporate all the latest gadgets into their design by fail horrible with their function. Don't get me wrong; design trends are important since they give us new techniques and inspiration. Implementing these styles and techniques must be focused and intelligent. Don't try to market on your blog. You need to focus on readability and usability instead of style. Websites that promote games need to feature graphics and things that give off a certain style and feel. Aesthetics are very important.

If a designer only uses a feel and look that works for one certain moment in time without giving any thought to how well it will function, the results will not be very effective.

Designing a website is about making an interface that is accessible, usable, and functions properly. It will also give off the correct feelings and emotions. All these elements are needed to get in touch with your businesses goals and stay in sync with your objectives. You need to identify these goals and use them to help with your design.

Here are some ways to help you think strategically about your website design:

Figure Out Your Goals

The first thing you should do before you start working on the design of your website is to know what your goals are. What do you want to achieve with this design? What is the purpose of the website? Ask yourself, a manager, or a client what these are. If you or they can't answer this question, you need to talk to someone until everything is agreed upon. Having clear directions is necessary if your design is to have a purpose.

Websites are works of art. It is an interface that is supposed to serve a certain function. This function might be selling products, delivering information, entertaining, informing or providing a service. Whatever the function is, the design needs to fulfill it. Goals are crucial if you start to work on a redesign. Why do you need a redesign? Are you looking to grow your sign-ups, increase participation, or decrease bounce rates?

Know Your Audience

The audience plays a huge role in how your site needs to function and look. A lot of different demographics will influence your design like technical competency, profession, gender, and age. A website for a serious business journal needs a style that is different than a computer game website. Usability plays a huge role for audiences that are less tech-savvy or older.

Your audience will influence the aesthetics of the site and will determine many of the little details such font size. You need to be clear about who could end up viewing your website.

Think About Brand Image

Many designers become overly inspired by the newest trends and start using them without thinking about what their image is and if it works for their brand. Reflective floors, gradients, and glossy buttons might work on some sites, but it may not for yours.

Think color. What feelings and emotions do you want to send to others? Your design needs to show the character and personality of your business. Everybody has their own brand. It doesn't matter if you sell a service or product, the website will have a certain feel that will make a good impression on visitors to your site. Figure out what that impression needs to be.

Goal-Driven Design

You have figured out the reasons behind your website, set your goals, figured out your audience and you know your image. Now you need to use it. How will you make sure your decisions work with your strategy? Look at it this way:

If the main objective is increasing how many subscribers your website gets. How could your design help you with this? There are three things that can help:

- Make your about section as concise and clear as you can. Don't confuse visitors about functions on your website.

- Use contrast and color to make a link that stands out. If they aren't able to find your registration link, you won't be able to get anyone to sign up.

- Make the process of registration easy by getting rid of optional and unnecessary elements. They can get to those later. If the form is too long, it will turn people away.

These are just some ways you can get your design to help you accomplish your goals by increasing how many people sign up for your services. Goals might change, but strategy stays the same. Focus and shape the design elements to meet these goals.

This strategy applies to your audience and brand. Design it to suit you. If your business is entertainment, then give your audience an "experience." You can use as much or as little imagery and color as you would like. If you are creating a website focused on information, your focus should be on readability and usability. The interface should fade away so that the user doesn't get distracted by the content.

New visitors might stay on the site for just a few seconds; you need to be concise, so you don't lose them. You can accomplish this by:

- Making use of large diagrams and imagery to how your service or product works.
- Show screenshots of the application process. People prefer to know what they are getting into before that choose to sign up.
- Give a tour. Show them the different way that your service can solve their problems. Post a video. The less effort it takes for people to understand and use your app the better.
- They need to be able to use the sign-up link on every page.

For your website to succeed it need to grab the attention of your visitors by educating and informing them quickly about your product and selling them on the benefits it gives.

Measure Your Results

After you have designed and posted your website, now you need to measure the success. This is important since you won't know how effective the design is until you test it out.

If you wanted to increase how many sign ups you get, measure to see if the changes made a positive impact. If your goal was to increase subscribers to your blog, you could check this by looking at RSS stats. If your goal was to increase involvement, check your comments to see if they have increased.

You could ask for feedback. This is the perfect way for you to see if you are going the right way. Just don't try to implement all the suggestions that people give you. Everybody has different tastes so everybody will also have different opinions about how the website should look. After you have collected feedback, check for patterns and see if you have any common issues that keep popping. Make these changes first.

Measuring website metrics is a complete science all by itself. It really doesn't matter how in-depth the analytics are right now, the main thing is you have some way to measure your objectives. Use the information to make sure your design is moving you in the right direction.

Kaizen

The Japanese philosophy of Kaizen puts the focus on small steps to continuously improve. When working on your website, think about Kaizen since what you just posted won't be your final version. You don't even need a final version.

You can constantly make improvements, and the way that a website works allows you to implement these at whatever time you need to. Since a website is not like a magazine that once it goes to print, you can't change anything or fix problems. With a website, it stays on your computer. If you screw something up, you can change it. You can also introduce improvements gradually and update your website to make it more efficient.

Using the measurement results, you will be able to see where the problem areas are. Your visitors might not be able to find the RSS link. You have a high bounce rate. You most important webpage isn't getting the right amount of traffic. It doesn't matter what the problem is, you can always fix it and improve on it.

Responsive Design

You need to make sure that your design can adjust from one device to another. This looks like a good approach, but it doesn't take into account images and text. What looks good on a desktop computer might be disastrous on mobile devices. Take your time and create a layout that works will every device. Remember to redesign images for small screens. A banner that has text might look great on a normal computer, but it might not be readable on a cell phone. You also don't want to use exactly the same images for a computer as a mobile device. The image will be scaled, but it will be larger than needed. It will increase how much bandwidth is used and how long it takes to load.

Software Prototyping

Using a graphics program like Adobe Edge Reflow to experiment with designs will help a great deal. When you have created a design that you love, you can copy the code to use with your actual layout.

A Team

You must have people that work well together. It is a good idea to have several team members if you have a lot of coding and design going on. A company I work with often has about 18 members so they can take on numerous projects at any time. This makes sure that all projects can be handled in a timely manner.

Versatility

Your team needs to be able to handle every aspect of graphic design and coding. They need to be easily accessible whether they work in an office or at home. This keeps you from being blindsided by someone that wants a certain type of job, and you don't have anyone who can do it. You will either have to run around to find support or turn the job down.

Customization

Utilizing templates might be tempting. These create a "look" that might appeal to you, especially if you deal with many corporate clients. By creating a look that is unique will make the client feel important since it helps with their branding.

Be Aware of the Marketplace

If you design for iOS, you won't have to build as many versions as you would for Android. This will simplify the process and lower cost.

Find Inspiration

You don't have to design in a vacuum. This actually makes designing harder. Look at websites that bring you inspiration. Study them and see what stands out to you. You can use these to build one of your own. You can also look for things that inspire you offline like in books and magazines. Find layout ideas that spark your creativity. When you are creating designs, be sure you do many different mockups for a client to look at. By doing this, you will have others they can choose from if they find one they don't like.

Take a Step Back

A good strategy is to step away from the screen. Most of the time, designers are working too close to their screen. Aside from the posture problems, this wreaks havoc with designs. Stepping away from the screen just for a few minutes or just moving your chair away from the desk will allow you to see the screen with different eyes. At times, elements that don't seem to go well together will look fine if you look at them from a distance. It is also a good idea to just walk away for a bit. When you come back to it, you will be able to look at it with a fresh perspective.

Start Your Design at a New Place

Most designers will start at the top of the page and work their way down. A different approach is to just experiment with blocks of design, text, and color. This makes the header just one of many components.

Test and Validate

Test your code, validate your code, and test the layout for the different devices and browsers that you have made the design for. For mobile devices, you need to turn the device sideways to see what happens to the layout.

To Sum It All Up

Everything on the web evolves. Remember that what works for this layout might not work for the next. Some design aspects won't change much and using them gives you a great foundation to start with.

The most important aspect of design work is to use common sense. You are designing something for someone who has a certain vision. It needs to fulfill that purpose. It is easy to get off track of your goals and to create something gorgeous, but it won't work within your context. It's also easy to fall into the latest trend trap, and only using things because they are pretty. These might not actually fit with what your project is about.

Try not to fall into the traps and think through each decision. Why is this button placed here?

What were the tabs for? Why are the icons there? If you can train your brain to work this way, the process becomes more focused. Keep in mind the organization or product you represent. Think about the brand or audience. What works in the context? What do they expect? How can design fulfill the vision of the website? Don't just make a pretty website, create that works for your customers.

Email Marketing

There are over 205 billion emails that are sent every day. This number is thought to increase to 246 billion by the year 2019. The strategies for email marketing has changed. The strategies that worked five years ago don't work now. It is still a great component of any marketing strategy. The best online marketers are still using email marketing as their go to. Why? It brings results and delivers the best return on investment.

You read that right. Email marketing does better than search engine optimization, pay per click, and content marketing all put together. Having a great email marketing strategy is the most important part of any marketing strategy. Email is the cheapest way to promote products, reach your goals, and talk to customers. For each dollar you spend on email marketing, you will get a return of $48. Pretty good, right? Here are five ways to use email marketing to get amazing results.

Personalize Messages

Personalized email marketing doesn't mean you send email to each subscriber. Personalization is using the customer's information to send messages personally. A great example of a company that personalizes email is Amazon. Every email from Amazon is personalized. It doesn't begin with Dear Customer. It starts with "Dear Sue." They don't randomly generate suggestions. They use your buying history to show you similar products.

With Amazon, email marketing isn't another marketing channel. It is the key to a great customer experience. Amazon's CEO is a genius when it comes to email marketing. He understands how valuable emails are and will read through any customer's complaints. This is why 35 percent of sales come from customer recommendations.

Amazon isn't the only company that gets these results by using personalization. Experian did a study and found that personalized emails gave them transaction rates that were six times higher.

Let's talk numbers anyone can understand. Most email marketing will generate about 11 cents for each email. If you send out 100,000 emails, you could see around $11,000 in sales. If you were to personalize the emails, you could get six times more back in returns. Now that's a great revenue opportunity.

Around 70 percent of businesses don't use personalized emails. If you personalize your emails, you could easily stand up against your competition and win. The easiest way to personalize your emails is addressing your recipient by name. Many email service providers offer this function. This alone will increase your company's performance. An email subject line with the recipient's name will increase rates by 16 percent.

If you consider that 47 percent of most emails are opened because what's in the subject line, this is a great way to get more eyes to your emails.

Here are other tips that you can use along with the customer's name to help you with personalization:

- Get the correct information, to begin with: Personalization begins before you ever hit the send button. It begins when a person fills out your sign up form. If you don't get their info like location, company, and name, you will be extremely limited when you try to personalize your communication attempts. Just ask for what you need instead of what you want. This is just one way that general data protection regulation will impact marketing.

- Use an email that they can reply to: If you use a donotreply@blah.com, it takes away any personalization from your messages. If you want your recipients to respond and be engaged, use a real reply address to improve your credibility to show that you are personable.

- Use your authentic email signature: This goes with using a real reply to email. You must use real contact information inside your email and give them the best way they can contact you. Give your recipients an opportunity to get in touch with you or connect with you online. It is a wonderful way to build relationships and get personal with them.

Segment Subscribers

Email marketers say that segmentation is next on the list of initiatives. When you segment your database, email campaigns will be targeted toward your audience.

Look at this example:

You want to host an event to network with small businesses that are located within a 20 miles radius around you. How do you get them to come to your event? Segmentation.

The easiest way to get the owners to come to your event is to create a segment of people that call themselves small business owners that live within your radius and send them an email invite.

Segmentation is simple and is done with customer relationship management software.

Think about sending emails to your whole database. You probably have subscribers all over the country possibly continent. How would you like to get an invitation to an event that is being held in another country? You probably wouldn't. Neither will they. Before you begin segmenting your database, let's see just how valuable it really is.

One study showed that all email marketing key performance indicators performed better when segmenting an email list. When you segment your lists, you will get more customers, better transactions, leads, revenue, and open rates. You may be asking if this really works? The answer is simply, yes.

If you send out two different email campaigns, both with the same subject line and content. The first was sent to a non-segmented list and the second was sent to a segmented list by interest. The non-segmented emails showed a 42 percent open rate and a 4.5 percent click-through rate. The segmented emails showed a 94 percent open rate and 38 percent click-through rate. That's pretty impressive. Is this why marketers segment their emails? No. Nine out of ten marketers don't segment their emails.

Here are some ways to get started with segmentation:

- Industry: Do you have products and services that other consumers and businesses could use? Knowing your subscriber's industry is the best way to segment your emails. If your business sells parts for cars, you would see a higher rate if you send emails to places that sell products for cars as compared to businesses that cell phones.

- Company size: Segmenting emails by annual revenue or company size is a wonderful way to increase rates. A business that only has five employees isn't going to want to go to a big industry conference, but a business who employs 750 people would be more likely to go to it.

- Sales cycle: Early buyers are not going to be ready for aggressive sales pitches or one on one demos, but they would appreciate receiving industry research on paper. On the other hand, buyers that are ready will respond to free trial offers or product webinars.

Send Emails that are Mobile Friendly

There is about 54 percent of the mobile users in the world who will open their email on their mobile devices. This is a fairly large number. What is the first thing you do in the morning? You reach for your phone and check it for email, messages, and missed calls.

About 62 percent of all mobile users do this. If you send an email to someone who opens it on their mobile devices, but the email hasn't been optimized for mobile devices, what are they going to do?

The first thing they will likely do is to unsubscribe and delete it. Why are half of all emails, not mobile friendly? When emails that are optimized for mobile devices generate much more revenue. The average revenue generated by mobile email is 40 cents per email. This is about four times greater than what desktop emails bring in.

Almost 55 percent of all smartphone users have purchased their mobile devices after receiving an email. About 36 percent of all business to business companies have optimized their emails to be viewed on mobile devices. They saw an improvement in the email performance.

How can you optimize your emails for mobile users?

- Implement responsive email design: Creating a RED design means the user's email is optimized no matter what device they are using. Most email service providers offer a solution in their email functions.

- Keep the pre-header and subject line short: Subject lines are critical. Keep it short, so the recipient knows what the email is about. The pre-header text shouldn't be wasted by saying "To view this email...." Try to summarize or use a call to action like giving them a coupon for free shipping.

- The Call to Action needs to be Obvious and Big: Mobile devices are all different sizes. If a text link works on a device with large screens, you could be alienating readers who have small devices or large hands. If you CTA is very small, make it bold, big, and easy to click.

Buttons, Design, and Test Copy

You need to test your email templates, landing page, and home pages. Testing gives you data to make decisions that improve your marketing performance. Email marketing isn't any different. You have tested subject lines, who hasn't.

If you send out different variations of the subject line to different subscribers, you can calculate the amount of revenue you can expect to receive. A sample revealed that the weakest line would generate about $400,000. The best line was thought to being $2,500,000. That is huge.

You can test other things by email marketing:

- From address: What appears in the form field has a great impact on if the reader will open the email or not. The sender name is the reason why the email gets opened. Test the *from address* by sending it from your CEO, company plus person, or just a person.

- HTML vs. Plain Text: Like many marketers, you send out plain texts of your emails. Have you ever thought of testing them as plain text only? When you add personalization, these emails look like they were written just for the recipient.

- Short vs. Long Emails: You have the option of sending out emails that are short or long. Long emails will include more detailed copies where short emails will send the recipient straight to a landing page. This way you can see which one works best.

Automate Emails When Possible

Trigger emails are sent out automatically based on the user's behavior. The most common are welcome, transactional, and thank you emails. Think about emails you get when you order something like order confirmation and receipts sent to your email. Trigger emails perform better than normal emails.

One study showed:

- Trigger emails open rates average about 49 percent. This is 95 percent higher than normal email.
- Trigger emails click-through rate is doubled when compared to normal email.
- Sites that convert about 40 percent of their traffic use trigger email.

Trigger-based email campaigns will generate four times more revenue and 18 times more profits. It does sound too good to be true. It has been tested, and it works.

About 25 percent of today's marketers use triggered emails and make up about 2.6 percent of the overall email volume. They are responsible for 20 percent of your revenue. Trigger emails work well since they hit an email marketing sweet spot.

Think about this:

You see an ad on social media and go to their website, you add an item to the cart but decide to leave before finishing the purchase. This happens a lot, every day. You check your email an hour later and have an email that shows the product you were thinking about buying along with a coupon for a ten percent discount plus free shipping. You are enticed to complete the purchase. This is the power of trigger emails.

Setting up triggered emails isn't that complex or expensive. You could start by using autoresponders with your customer service software.

Here are examples of trigger emails you can use:

- Activation: A user creates an account but doesn't come back to your site within a week. You can create an activation campaign that will send automated emails with their information along with steps on how to get started. You can even include a video to demonstrate for added support. Invite them to a meeting and walk them through any problems they may be having. Answer their questions in a timely manner.

- Win-back: A customer is getting near the end of their subscription. They haven't used the product for the past three months, and you need to get them back and keep them for one more year. Make a win-back email that will send automated emails to every customer that is coming to the end of their contract. Give them a list of new products and features along with a short plan of expected releases within the next few months.

- Surprise: Loyal customers are the key to success. You should reward your loyal customers by offering free products or services. Send them a surprise email that offers them a coupon for free doughnuts, cupcakes, gift cards, or even a free year to your software. It is a cost for the company, but the rewards will be big.

Email marketing will deliver results. Email marketing has evolved over the years. It isn't just as simple as sending the exact same email to everyone. You need to update your marketing strategy. You need to send targeted messages. Personalized messages that can be opened on any device.

Test new elements. Trends quickly change and what worked last month may not work today. When you have figured out what works, find a way to automate with triggered emails.

When you can make these new changes, your customers will become more responsive. Your performance will improve, and you will see your business grow.

The Best Time to Send Emails

There are numerous emails sent out during business hours, the ones that have the best open rates are not sent between 9 am and 5 pm. The best email strategy is to send emails at night. These emails should be sent between 8 pm and midnight. This block outperforms all times for open rates, click-throughs, and sales. This window is not used as much, and this helps the late night emails outperform.

The time for optimal mailing will depend on the consumer's behavior, inbox crowding, and when other marketers send out their emails.

Deployment times and inbox crowding of marketers go hand in hand. If your email gets sent out at times when there aren't many others sent, it will have a better chance of being seen.

Optimal emailing to customers is totally up to you. Do a lot of testing and figure out how your customers tick and when they open their email.

Email is Used More than Twitter and Facebook

Social media might be nipping on email's heels, but the inbox still holds its own to social influence. SocialTwist did a study over an 18-month time frame. They monitored 119 campaigns from leading companies and brands.

Their results showed an advantage to the ability of email to get new customers as compared to Twitter and Facebook.

Out of the 300,000 people that became customers, 50.8 percent was gotten through email. Twitter reached 26.8 percent, and Facebook gained 22 percent.

Email rules by double. Mailchimp, Aweber, and Constant Contact are a few email marketing service providers with intuitive platforms.

Email on the Weekend

Sending emails on Saturday and Sunday outperform any weekday emails. The amount of email that is sent over the weekend is low just like the late evening email. These can help your messages stand out even more. The rates for sales, open, and click through aren't substantial, but in marketing, every bit counts.

Online Promotions

To be able to increase your business's growth, you must increase people's awareness and get them engaged online. Using promotions like sweepstakes, giveaways, and contest are the best tools you could use to build excitement about your business. It can also help you build better relationships with existing and potential customers in miraculous ways.

Here are some tips to make sure your next promotion is a rousing success:

- Make Participations Very Easy: If you can make it extremely easy for people to get involved with your promotions, and the prizes are exceptional, they will get involved quicker. To get the best participation, get rid of all the barriers you can. Making them jump through hoops like making them create an account or the entry form is numerous pages long will decrease the chances of them entering. Remember the old adage, keep it simple. Creating a promotion that is complex might seem like fun for you, but for customers, the easier the process, the more people you will attract.
- Share Photos: By placing photos in your promotion is a great way to get your

audience engaged. Consumers enjoy looking at photos when spending time with friends whether it is in person or on social media. Potential clients will engage faster with businesses if they place photos on their site. People love to look at photos. They also love to show off their skills. Increase their engagement by letting them share a photo as a way to enter your contest.

- Promotions Need to be Mobile-Friendly: Around 66 percent of promotions are viewed on mobile devices. Since most people use their mobile devices and smartphones for everything, you need to think about how your promotion will look on all mobile devices. You can't just shrink it to fit; you must adapt it to work on all mobile devices. Some platforms can detect what browser is being used and will optimize your promotion for each device.

- Use Word-of-Mouth to Fuel Your Promotion: For each person that entered a competition, there were 3.6 more people who entered due to social sharing. Ask your staff and clients to share the promotion on the social media they use. Contests on Twitter asks users to retweet the contest as a way to enter, and this shares the contest with other Twitter users. Offer your staff click-to-tweets to get awareness out there quickly and easily. If you are promoting on

Facebook, do the same thing with a share button. Just remember to add a disclosure if your employees share.

- Supercharge the Promotion by Using Paid Media: You must invest in your promotion to succeed. Use the leverage of Facebook's promoted posts, sponsored stories, and ads. This is an affordable and great way to reach farther than just the people who are already following you. Paid StumbleUpon ads, LinkedIn ads, and promoted tweets will increase participation. Paid media can increase participation by about 55 percent and lowers the cost per entry by about 42 percent.

Using social media to bring awareness to your promotion are key for any marketer. Get the most out of them by making sure they are mobile, promoted, shareable, engaging, and simple. Remember to optimize your reach by increasing your chances of people talking about it. Most important, make sure you are worthy of being talked about.

Conclusion

I would like to thank you once again for purchasing my book.

Wouldn't it be wonderful if you could work at your convenience and do things that you genuinely enjoy? You no longer have to sit at a desk and work on something that doesn't interest you. Web businesses are lucrative and exciting. All you need to do is think of an avenue that interests you and get started with your own business! Make use of the information provided in this book to find something that suits your needs. You don't have to stick to just one of the avenues mentioned in this book. You can create multiple streams of income if you want to. Once you have finalized on an idea, the next step is to implement it. All the hard work, effort, and time you put into will be indeed worth it! Take control of your life today and become your own boss!

I really hope you enjoyed this book and it helps you as you begin your exciting journey toward starting your own online business. I would greatly appreciate it if you left my book a review; it really helps indie authors, like myself, out. Thank you so much, my readers truly mean the world to me.

Contact Information:

julie@jrpublishinggroup.com

Website:

www.julierausch.wix.com/author

Please sign up below for my newsletter to receive tips, resources, and **FREEBIES**!

Please go to this link for free offer:

"Easy Marketing Tips for Your Home-Based Business"

http://eepurl.com/c8rgw5

Or visit my website:

www.julierausch.wix.com/author

To sign up

www.ingramcontent.com/pod-product-compliance
Lightning Source LLC
Chambersburg PA
CBHW031420210526
45464CB00005B/1979